# HOW TO MA.I.M. A MOCKINGBIRD

ESPIONAGE LOGISTICS DIRECTORATE • STRATEGIC HAZARD INTERVENTION

# HOW TO MA.I.M. A MOCKINGBIRD

NFANTRY> > > COLLAPSE

WRITERS: **NICK SPENCER** & **ALES KOT**
ARTIST, #12-14: **BUTCH GUICE**
ARTIST, #15-16: **LUKE ROSS**
COLOR ARTIST: **MATTHEW WILSON**
INKERS: **TOM PALMER** (#13) & **JOE RUBINSTEIN** (#13-14)
LETTERER: **VC'S CLAYTON COWLES**
COVER ART: **BUTCH GUICE** & **MATTHEW WILSON**
ASSISTANT EDITORS: **JON MOISAN** EDITOR: **LAUREN SANKOVITCH**
EXECUTIVE EDITOR: **TOM BREVOORT**

ARTILLERY> > > COLLAPSE

COLLECTION EDITOR: **SARAH BRUNSTAD**
ASSOCIATE MANAGING EDITOR: **ALEX STARBUCK**
EDITOR, SPECIAL PROJECTS: **MARK D. BEAZLEY & JENNIFER GRÜNWALD**
SENIOR EDITOR, SPECIAL PROJECTS: **JEFF YOUNGQUIST**
SVP PRINT, SALES & MARKETING: **DAVID GABRIEL** BOOK DESIGNER: **NELSON RIBEIRO**

EDITOR IN CHIEF: **AXEL ALONSO** CHIEF CREATIVE OFFICER: **JOE QUESADA**
PUBLISHER: **DAN BUCKLEY** EXECUTIVE PRODUCER: **ALAN FINE**

LOGISTICS> > > COLLAPSE

**CRET AVENGERS VOL. 3: HOW TO MA.I.M. A MOCKINGBIRD.** Contains material originally published in magazine form as SECRET AVENGERS #12-16. First printing 2014. ISBN# 978-0-785 32-9. Published by MARVEL WORLDWIDE, INC., a subsidiary of MARVEL ENTERTAINMENT, LLC. OFFICE OF PUBLICATION: 135 West 50th Street, New York, NY 10020.  **Printed in Canada.** ALAN FINE, EVP - Office of the President, Marvel Worldwide, Inc. and EVP & CMO Marvel Characters B.V.; DAN BUCKLEY, Publish President - Print, Animation & Digital Divisions; JOE QUESADA, Chief Creative Officer; TOM BREVOORT, SVP of Publishing; DAVID BOGART, SVP of Operations & Procurement, Publishin 3. CEBULSKI, SVP of Creator & Content Development; DAVID GABRIEL, SVP Print, Sales & Marketing; JIM O'KEEFE, VP of Operations & Logistics; DAN CARR, Executive Director of Publishir chnology; SUSAN CRESPI, Editorial Operations Manager; ALEX MORALES, Publishing Operations Manager; STAN LEE, Chairman Emeritus. For information regarding advertising in Marv mics or on Marvel.com, please contact Niza Disla, Director of Marvel Partnerships, at ndisla@marvel.com. For Marvel subscription inquiries, please call 800-217-9158. **Manufactured betwee 28/2014 and 4/7/2014 by SOLISCO PRINTERS, SCOTT, QC, CANADA.**

9 8 7 6 5 4 3 2 1

HOW TO MA.I.M.
A MOCKINGBIRD
PART ONE
SECRET
AVENGERS

# SECRET AVENGERS

CHAIN OF COMMAND > > > COLLAPSE

**MARIA HILL**
*DIRECTOR OF S.H.I.E.L.D.*

**NICK FURY**
*FIELD AGENT*

**PHIL COULSON**
*TACTICAL SUPPORT*

**HAWKEYE**
*CLINT BARTON*
*MARKSMAN/ASSET*

**BLACK WIDOW**
*NATASHA ROMANOFF*
*EX-KGB SPY/ASSET*

**MOCKINGBIRD**
*BOBBI MORSE*
*FIELD AGENT/ASSET*

**IRON PATRIOT**
*LT-COL JAMES RHODES*
*ARMORED TACTICAL/ASSET*

**HULK**
*BRUCE BANNER*
*HEAVY ORDNANCE/ASSET*

**TASKMASTER**
*TONY MASTERS*
*DOUBLE AGENT/ASSET*

MISSION NOTES > > > COLLAPSE

IN THE WAKE OF AN ASSASSINATION ATTEMPT AGAINST THE FORMER TERRORIST ORGANIZATION A.I.M. GONE AWRY, NEWLY REINSTALLED DIRECTOR OF S.H.I.E.L.D. MARIA HILL HAD TO NAVIGATE A POLITICAL FIRESTORM THAT COULD HAVE GRAVE INTERNATIONAL CONSEQUENCES FOR HER COVERT SECRET AVENGERS SQUAD AND S.H.I.E.L.D. ITSELF. WHILE AGENTS BLACK WIDOW, HAWKEYE AND NICK FURY MADE IT HOME, MOCKINGBIRD WAS COMPROMISED AND REMAINS IN HIDING ON A.I.M. ISLAND, WITH NO MEMORY OF HER REAL MISSION. UNFORTUNATELY, MOCKINGBIRD'S MEMORY WIPE LEFT HER MOSTLY AMNESIAC ABOUT EVEN HER ACTUAL IDENTITY. ATTEMPTING TO STAY UNDETECTED AND UNDERCOVER AS AN A.I.M. AGENT, MOCKINGBIRD'S LUCK RAN OUT WHEN HER BORROWED PERSONA WAS CALLED IN FRONT OF THE A.I.M. HIGH COUNCIL FOR A PRESENTATION...

THE PROJECT IS MOVING FORWARD...IN A POSITIVE, STRAIGHTFORWARD DIRECTION.

FORWARD. STRAIGHTFORWARD. I'M BOTCHING THIS UP ALREADY.

THIS IS BAD

BARBUDA.
A.I.M. ISLAND.

THE MINOR IRRITATIONS ALONG THE WAY ARE NOW *FULLY RESOLVED.*

MAKE IT UP AS YOU GO ALONG. MAKE IT UP AS YOU GO ALONG. COME ON, BOBBI.

BOBBI MORSE, a.k.a
MOCKINGBIRD

SECRET AVENGER. WORKS FOR S.H.I.E.L.D. DEEEEEEEEEP COVER.

IT IS UNBALANCED.
BUY TIME.

I DON'T REALLY GET IT.

WHAT DO I KNOW.
BUY TIME.

IT'S SIMPLE.

IN LAYMAN'S TERMS, THE EXTREMIS TECHNOLOGY REFUSES TO BE REPLICATED BECAUSE WE HAVE JUST A SLIVER OF THE NECESSARY DATA.
HOWEVER, THE TANGENTIAL NANOBOT RESEARCH HAS POTENTIAL, ESPECIALLY IF WE CONSIDER ITS IMPLICATIONS AS A RESILIENT TECHNOLOGY.

UH. YEAH. LAYMAN'S TERMS.

EXTREMIS AND A.I.M. NANOBOTS.
POTENTIAL.
DUTY. PRIDE. SCIENCE. IMPRESS THEM.
DEAR COUNCIL, I AM HEREBY ASKING YOU FOR FORTY-EIGHT MORE HOURS.
IMPRESS THEM AND GET THE HELL OUT OF THIS PLACE.

I FIRMLY BELIEVE WE ARE ON THE VERGE OF A BREAKTHROUGH WITH THE NANOBOTS.
THE POTENTIAL OF THE TECHNOLOGY IS ASTOUNDING-- WE JUST REQUIRE A LITTLE MORE TIME TO MAKE SURE THE TECH IS IMPENETRABLE.
A.I.M. DUTY. PRIDE.
APPEAL TO IT.
IF WE FAIL, I WILL TAKE FULL RESPONSIBILITY. I WILL END MY LIFE RIGHT IN FRONT OF YOU.
IN THE NAME OF SCIENCE, I ASK FOR TWO MORE DAYS.

I DO NOT ENDORSE THIS.
COME ON...

HE ASKED FOR TWO DAYS, NOT TWO YEARS...
GIVE ME A YES.

TWO DAYS AND TWO YEARS ARE ONE AND THE SAME THING. TIME IS THE DUNG FROM WHICH IDEAS SPROUT TO LIFE. ACCELERATE THE DUNG.

SURE, BOBBI.
AH. GOOD.

TWO DAYS IN AN INTERROGATION CELL.
WAIT, *WHAT?*

S.H.I.E.L.D. HELICARRIER ILIAD.
"DIRECTOR HILL.
"CAN I HAVE YOUR ATTENTION FOR A MOMENT?"

A MOMENT?
A FEW. MOMENTS. POSSIBLY.
MAYBE LONGER.

IS THIS ABOUT DAISY JOHNSON?
NOT REALLY.
NOT REALLY OR NOT AT ALL?
NOT AT ALL.
WHY AM I INTERESTED IN THIS, COULSON?

BECAUSE I AM A GOOD AGENT AND YOU TRUST ME?
HERE'S YOUR COOKIE.

...
THERE IS NO COOKIE.

I KNOW. WELCOME TO S.H.I.E.L.D. WHAT DO YOU WANT?

# HOW TO MA.I.M. A MOCKINGBIRD

PART ONE OF FIVE

WE COME IN PEACE.

SERIOUSLY?
TRIPLE-SCANNED. ALL CLEAR.

YOU. YOU HAVE *ONE* MINUTE OF MY TIME. CONVINCE ME THAT I DON'T WANT TO THROW YOU IN GUANTANAMO.

WE ARE JUST THE FIRST WAVE.
OUR LEADER WILL COME ONLY IF HE UNDERSTANDS THAT YOU LET US GO.

FORSON?
NO. NO. OUR *TRUE* LEADER WILL REVEAL HIMSELF IN DUE TIME.
THIRTY SECONDS.

THESE ARE THE LOCATIONS OF SIX HIDDEN A.I.M. BASES THAT ARE DEVELOPING SECRET WEAPONRY.

...YES, OF COURSE I CAN REPEAT IT FOR YOUR PRECAMBRIAN CAMERA.
ANDREW FORSON IS THE PROBLEM.
AND YOU WANT WORLD PEACE.
YES.
HELICARRIER, INTERROGATION ROOM.

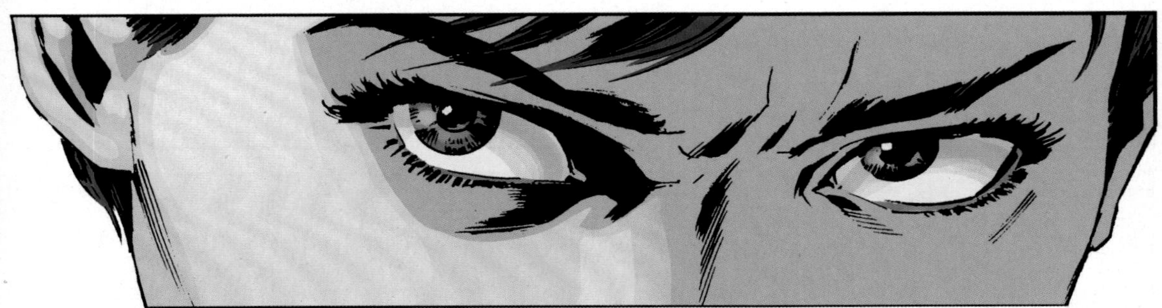

JUST JOKING.
WE ARE VERY HIGH ABOVE THE GROUND. I CAN KICK YOU OUT OF THE HELICARRIER RIGHT NOW AND YOU WILL FALL A LONG WAY AND YOU WILL WATCH YOUR MISERABLE LIFE PLAY OUT IN FRONT OF YOU AS YOU FALL TO CERTAIN DEATH.

THIS IS WHAT HAPPENS IF YOU MAKE MORE "JOKES."

WE...

...WE WOULD SIMPLY PREFER THE OLD ARRANGEMENT.
WITH SOME NEW ADJUSTMENTS.

NEW ADJUSTMENTS.
YES.
SUCH AS?
WE WANT TO WORK WITH YOU. WITH S.H.I.E.L.D.
KIND OF LIKE THE NAZI SCIENTISTS COLLABORATING WITH THE UNITED STATES AFTER THE SECOND WORLD WAR.
YOU'RE NOT AS TALENTED.
OUCH.
LET'S SAY IT COULD HAPPEN. I AM NOT SAYING IT WILL. WHAT WOULD YOU GIVE ME AS A GESTURE OF GOOD FAITH?
HOW ABOUT AN UNDERWATER BASE CALLED MEDUSA THAT IS CURRENTLY USED AS A TRAINING CENTER FOR FORSON'S BLACK GUARD?

A.I.M. ISLAND.
FORSON KNEW ABOUT HER AND HE DIDN'T SHARE THIS WITH US. HE'S BECOMING A RECKLESS OPERATOR. THIS COULD HAVE COST US. THIS COULD HAVE COST EVERYONE.

I KNEW.

OF COURSE YOU DID...

WHY KEEP THIS FROM US?
I SAW THE OUTCOME.

THEN NO HARM DONE, RIGHT?

...RIGHT?

BOBBI...
HOW MUCH DO YOU REMEMBER?
NOTHING.

TASKMASTER.
YES, THAT IS WHO I AM.
I AM THE TASK--
WE HAVE NO TIME FOR THIS. I KNOW WHO YOU ARE. YOU KNOW WHO I AM.
ACTUALLY I DON--
AGENT COULSON.
OH. YES. YOU.
HI.
WHERE'S HILL?
BUSY.
DOES SHE KNOW WHAT'S HAPPENING OVER HERE?
THAT DEPENDS. WHAT IS HAPPENING?
MOCKINGBIRD...
SHE KNOWS ABOUT THAT.
WHICH IS WHY I'M TALKING TO YOU.
IT'S TIME TO GET OFF THE ISLAND.
OKAY.
JUST GOTTA STRETCH FIRST.
CAUTION

MENTALLO.
I SENSE HESITATION INSIDE YOU.

WHAT?
NO...
WHAT SORTA HESITATION DO YOU MEAN?

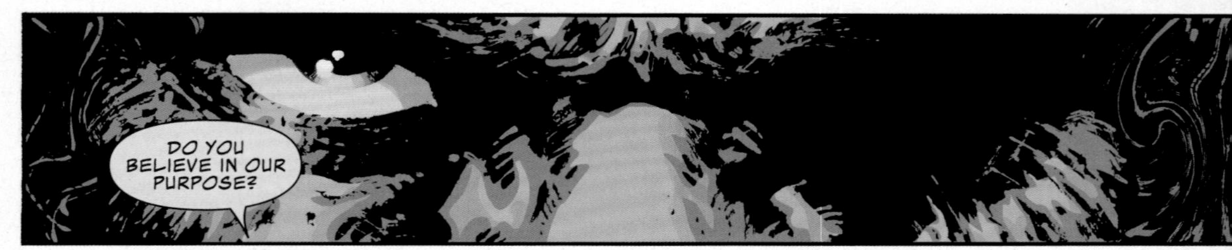
DO YOU BELIEVE IN OUR PURPOSE?

MAN...OR WHATEVER YOU ARE, JUDE...
...THAT'S A LOADED QUESTION.

I BELIEVE STUFF JUST... SORTA HAPPENS, YOU KNOW?

IT'S A CHANCE TO DO SOMETHING COOL. HAVE FUN. LIVE A LITTLE.

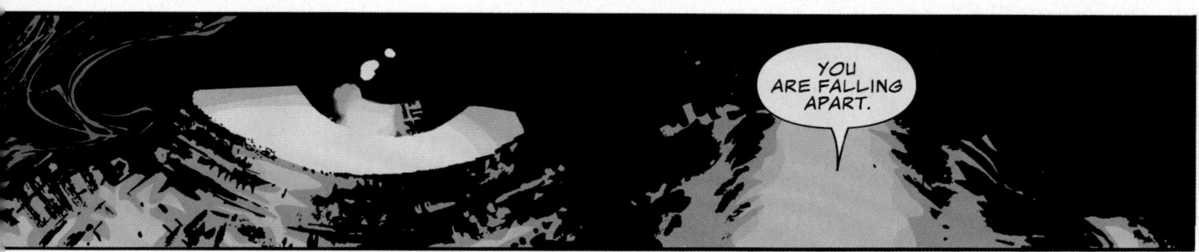
YOU ARE FALLING APART.

YEAH. MAYBE A LITTLE.
DON'T SPEED UP THE PROCESS, ALL RIGHT?

I LIKE THE SUNSETS HERE.

THE A.I.M. BASE *MEDUSA.*
111 MILES OFF THE COAST OF BARBUDA.

TORPEDO SHAFT.

EMERGENCY EXIT T-5.

HAWKEYE IN POSITION. ALL CLEAR.

SHANG-CHI? BROTHER, WHAT ARE YOU DOING H--

--HHHHEERRE.
OKAY.

HAWKEYE?
I REPEAT. **HAWKEYE?**

HAWKEYE, REPLY--
FURY--

PLEASE.
BE UNREASONABLE AND FIGHT US.
YELENA BELOVA,
A.I.M. MINISTER OF DEFENSE.

UNREASONABLE?

I DON'T DO EMOTIONS. I'M A SPY, NOT AN ACTOR.

S.H.I.E.L.D. HELICARRIER ILIAD.
OUR COMMANDER-IN-CHIEF WILL BE VERY PLEASED TO MEET YOU, DIRECTOR HILL.
WE HAVE A PROBLEM. A MEDUSA BASE-EXPLORATION MISSION PROBLEM.
HOW BAD?
MAGIC WORD TIME BAD.
WAIT FOR ME.
KERUNK
I'LL BE WITH YOU IN FIVE---
WHRRRRRRCLANK
AW, HELL...
Scitterscitterscitter

DIRECTOR HILL.
LET'S TALK BUSINESS.
M.O.D.O.K.
DOES WHATEVER A M.O.D.O.K.* CAN.
*S.H.I.E.L.D. ARCHIVES: MENTAL ORGANISM DESIGNED ONLY FOR KILLING. SERIOUSLY.

HOW TO MA.I.M.
A MOCKINGBIRD
PART TWO
SECRET
AVENGERS

I.M. ADAPTOID
PERATIONS
ENTER.

I'M BEATING UP HAWKEYE!
THIS IS *AWESOME!*

THIS IS THE *REAL* ROBERTO KOWALSKI!

I'M A *BIG* MAN!
YEAH!

WANNA TRY?
EH...
SURE. WHY NOT.

MENTALLO.
MINISTER OF PUBLIC AFFAIRS.

...IT'S NOT DOING WHAT I WANT.
UH...
YEAH. THE ADAPTOID ONLY ALLOWS YOU TO MOVE IT IN CLEAR SPOTS-- MEANING ONLY WHEN IT'S SURE IT'S OUT OF DANGER...

...LIKE RIGHT NOW.
FINISH HIM.
JUST THINK ABOUT THE MOVE AND HIT HIM HARD.

FATALITY!

I MEAN, NOT REALLY, I HOPE.
THE ORDERS SAID TO BRING ALL OF THEM BACK ALIVE...

WHAT IS THIS GOOD FOR AGAIN...?

ELSEWHERE.

ARE YOU FULLY COMMITTED TO OUR TASK?

I-I AM, TASKMASTER.

TASKMASTER.
MINISTER OF DEFENSE.

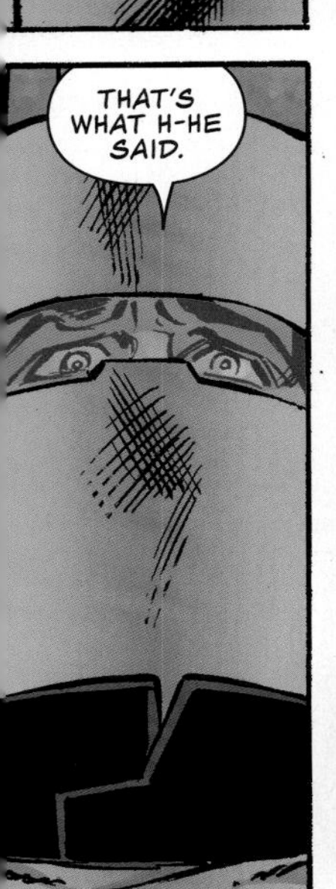

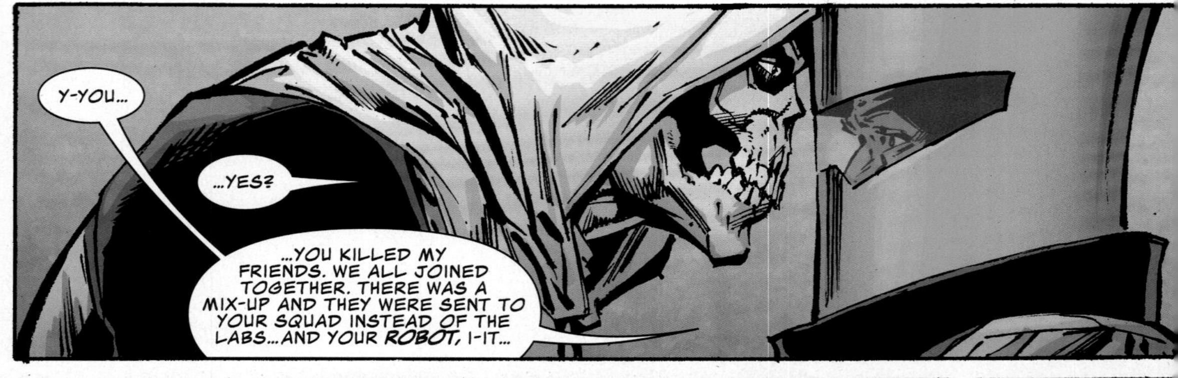

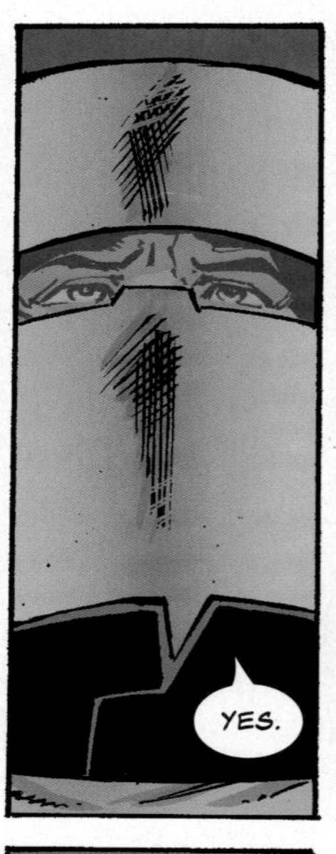

# HOW TO MA.I.M. A MOCKINGBIRD

PART TWO OF FIVE

S.H.I.E.L.D. HELICARRIER ILIAD.
INTERROGATION ROOM 999.
DID YOU KNOW THAT THE MEDUSA BASE WAS A TRAP?
NO.
WHY WOULD I BELIEVE YOU?
BECAUSE I WOULDN'T WALK STRAIGHT INTO YOUR ARMS IF THAT WERE THE CASE. SOMEONE OBVIOUSLY CHANGED THE PROTOCOL.
MARIA HILL.
RUNS THE S.H.I.E.L.D.
M.O.D.O.K.
WORKED FOR A.I.M.-- NOW A TRAITOR TO THE CAUSE.
OU KNOW WHAT THAT TELLS ME?
THAT TELLS ME YOUR DATA AIN'T WORTH MUCH. OR THAT IT'S COMPROMISED.
THE DATA. IS WORTH. BILLIONS.
I SWEAR ON MY MOTHER'S GRAVE.
I DIDN'T KNOW YOU HAD A MOTHER.
I DID.

BUT THIS ISN'T ABOUT ME PLAYING YOU EMOTIONALLY SO YOU CAN GIVE ME WHAT I WANT.
I AM HERE TO CONDUCT BUSINESS. I KNOW YOU ARE TOO SMART TO PLAY MY GAMES.
SO YOU'RE SWITCHING FROM THE EMOTIONALLY CHARGED TACTICS ABOUT A DEAD MOTHER--BECAUSE YOU'VE DONE YOUR RESEARCH ON ME AND KNOW I RECENTLY LOST MINE--TO GENTLY BUT FIRMLY ENCOURAGING MY INTELLIGENCE?
YOU'RE AN EXTRAORDINARILY HORRIBLE PICKUP ARTIST, M.O.D.O.K.
*S.H.I.E.L.D. ARCHIVES: MENTAL ORGANISM DESIGNED ONLY FOR KILLING.
ANDREW FORSON IS NOT GOOD FOR A.I.M. HE'S BAD. BAD BAD BAD.
AH. FINALLY.

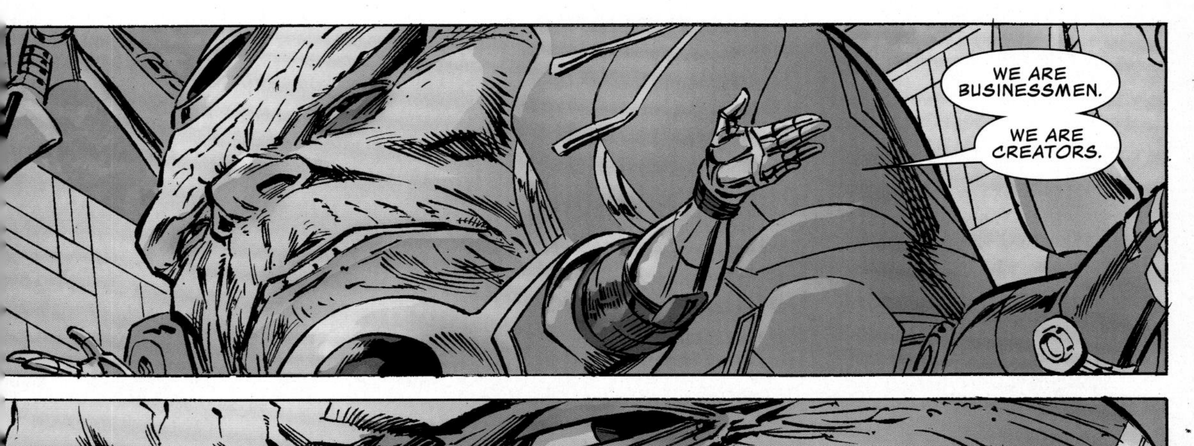
WE ARE BUSINESSMEN.
WE ARE CREATORS.

WE'RE NOT RELIGIOUS FANATICS.

ONCE UPON A TIME, A.I.M. KNEW ITS PLACE...

I TAKE IT YOU'RE TALKING ABOUT ***THE ENTROPY CULT?***

...BUT THE LANDSCAPE ***CHANGED.*** RELIGIOUS ZEALOTS ARE TAKING ADVANTAGE OF THE UNSCIENTIFICALLY MINDED WITHIN OUR COMMUNITY...

...FORSON MUST ***GO.***

HAVE I DONE WELL, SIR?
YOU'RE A NATURAL, SON.
TESS-ONE IS WELL-OILED. THIS IS A SURPRISE FIGHT THEY WILL NEVER FORGET.
A.I.M. ISLAND.
YOUR FIRST TEST IS A RAGING SUCCESS.
RIGHT BEHI--
I
KNOW
BUT
THANK
YOU.

DID YOU FORGET TO TELL THEM THAT THIS WASN'T A STANDARD EXERCISE AND THAT THEY WERE FORBIDDEN TO ATTEMPT ATTACKING ME THIS TIME?

UH...

I AM A FORGIVING TEACHER, MY DEAR APPRENTICE.

FOR THIS TRANSGRESSION, I WILL SIMPLY CALL YOU TODD.

BUT MY NAME--

IS NOW TODD.

THE CHARIOT.
COVERT A.I.M. RESEARCH FACILITY. ST. PETERSBURG, RUSSIA.
M.O.D.O.K. WAS RIGHT. THIS BASE IS FULL OF A.I.M. GOODIES.
HOW DO WE WANT TO MOVE ALL THIS TECH FROM RUSSIA, COULSON?
I LIKE THE IDEA OF TELEPORTING IT BIT BY BIT, DR. BANNER. LET ME CHECK ON THAT WITH DIRECTOR HILL...
COULD WE GET DOCTOR STRANGE TO DO THE TELEPORTING THING? I ALWAYS WANTED TO SPEND MORE TIME AROUND THE GUY. FIGURE OUT THE MAGIC...
"ANY SUFFICIENTLY ADVANCED TECHNOLOGY IS INDISTINGUISHABLE FROM MAGIC," RHODEY.
DID YOU JUST CALL DOCTOR STRANGE A SCIENTIST?
PRETTY MUCH.

RHODEY! BANNER! ARE YOU THERE?
TALK TO ME!

METAL... MAN...OKAY?
HULK... SAVE?

MY HERO.

PERFECT.
DR. ANDREW FORSON.
A.I.M. SCIENTIST SUPREME.
WHY ARE YOU GRINNING LIKE A MAGGOT THAT JUST DISCOVERED A FRESH CORPSE?
BECAUSE I JUST KILLED--OR AT LEAST SERIOUSLY INJURED--TWO AVENGERS WITH NOTHING BUT MY BRAIN AND A FINGER.
BECAUSE WE HAVE DISCOVERED THE TRAITOR IN OUR MIDST.
BECAUSE BELOVA IS BRINGING BACK ANOTHER THREE AVENGERS.
SUPERIA.
MINISTER OF EDUCATION.
"BECAUSE THE PLAN IS WORKING."

ALL I'M SAYING IS, AT LEAST I LOOK LIKE I PUT UP A FIGHT.
OW. TALKING *HURTS.*

AND PUTTING UP A FIGHT HELPED YOU HOW EXACTLY, HAWKEYE?

IT HELPED ME FEEL LIKE I DIDN'T JUST *GIVE UP,* FURY--

YOU THINK GIVING UP IS ALWAYS A BAD THING? YOU'D MAKE *THE WORST SPY* EVER--
BOYS--

CAN YOU STOP MEASURING YOUR SPECIAL PARTS AND SAVE THE *ENERGY* FOR WHEN YOU'LL *NEED* IT?

WHY IS SHANG-CHI HELPING THEM, ANYWAY?
THAT AIN'T SHANG-CHI.

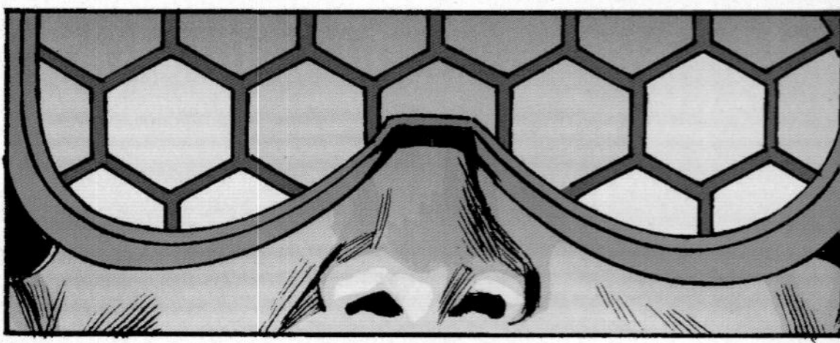

"I WAS ALWAYS ON YOUR SIDE..."

...I JUST HAD TO WAIT FOR THE RIGHT MOMENT. BUT YOU CAN TALK TO ME, MOCKINGBIRD. I MEAN, I GOT YOU OUT. IT'S PRETTY CLEAR WHOSE SIDE I'M ON.
COME ON. TIME TO SAY GOODBYE TO THE ISLAND.
WHAT HAPPENED TO YOU, BOBBI...?

MY NAME IS NOT TODD.

IT'S *ANTON TRASK.*

AND I AM NO ONE'S APPRENTICE.

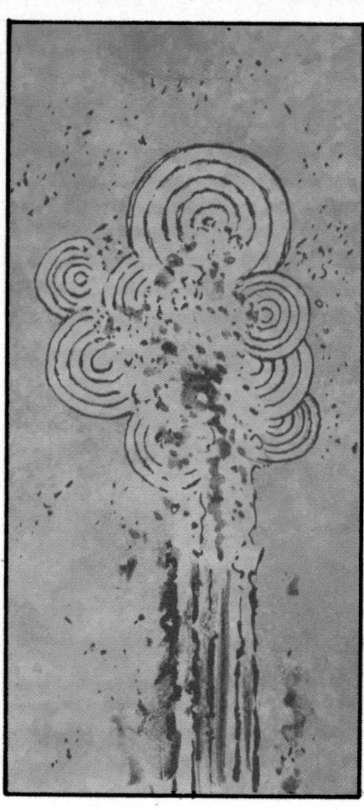

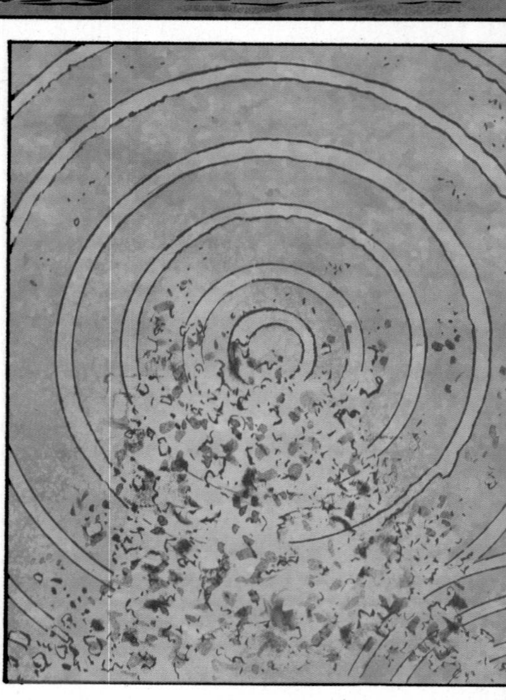

I WILL SHOOT YOU RIGHT NOW.

THAT WOULD BE A VIOLATION OF ABOUT 30 DIFFERENT LAWS--
I DON'T CARE.
I HAD NOTHING TO DO WITH THIS. AND YOU WON'T SHOOT ME.

I HAD NO IDEA FORSON WAS SO WELL-PREPARED. THIS IS NOT ME TRYING TO TRICK YOU INTO LOSING YOUR AGENTS. IF I WANTED TO DO THAT, I COULD HAVE DONE IT BY PROXY.

YOU NEARLY COST ME TWO AGENTS. AND ANOTHER THREE ARE IN DANGER.

NO. YOU ARE NOT SENDING MORE AGENTS WITH THEM BECAUSE YOU WANTED A FAST AND LEAN RESPONSE--THAT'S WHAT DID IT. NOT JUST MY INFORMATION. YOU RUSHED IN BECAUSE YOU WERE TOO EAGER TO HIT FORSON HARD.

ROOKIE.

LET'S WORK TOGETHER. YOU CAN HOOK ME UP TO A LIE DETECTOR RIGHT NOW. I AM TELLING THE TRUTH.
HOW DO I KNOW YOU'RE GOING TO DELIVER?
GIVE ME SOMETHING THAT WILL GIVE US A REAL, IMMEDIATE ADVANTAGE AND WE CAN CONTINUE TALKING.
YOU DON'T.

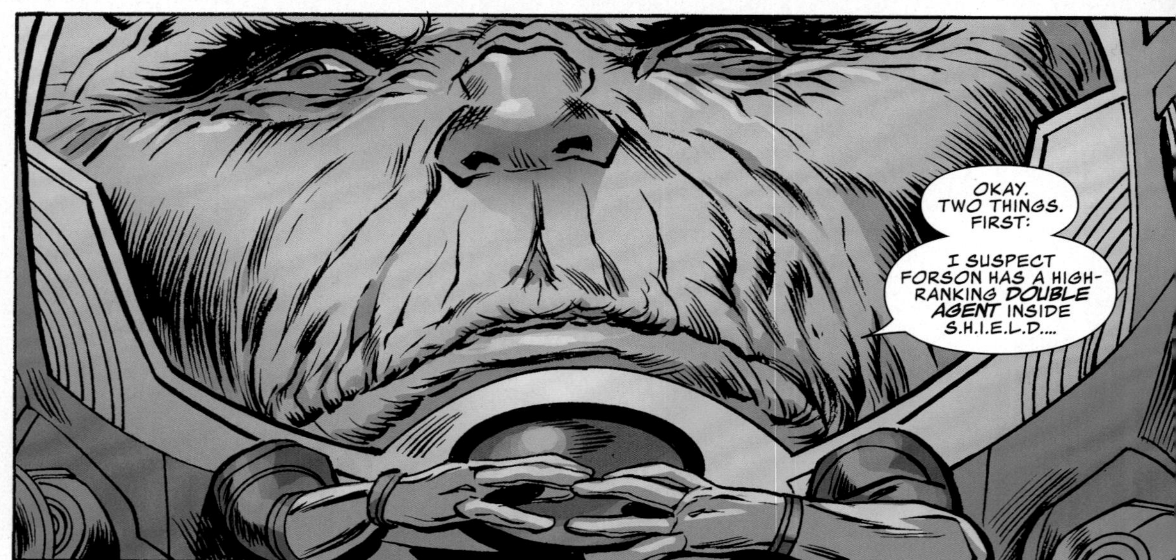
OKAY. TWO THINGS. FIRST:
I SUSPECT FORSON HAS A HIGH-RANKING DOUBLE AGENT INSIDE S.H.I.E.L.D....

ABOUT A YEAR AGO, BEFORE HE EVEN GOT ALL THE WAY UP WHERE HE IS NOW, HE WAS RUNNING TESTS ON SOME NEW BLACK MARKET MIND-WIPING TECH THAT COULD ERASE YOUR MIND WITH A TRIGGER WORD, AND I SUSPECTED HE EMPLOYED SIMILAR MEANS LONG BEFORE THEN...

THIS IS OBVIOUSLY A *HUGE* MISTAKE.
"...I ALSO SUSPECT HE TURNED THE TASKMASTER LONG BEFORE YOU GOT TO HIM."
OBVIOUSLY.
NO WALLS CAN HOLD ME.
OF COURSE.
MOCKINGBIRD WILL *TEAR* THROUGH THIS PLACE, TOO.
"AND SECOND..."

BLAM!
"SO LET'S CLEAN UP BEFORE SOMEONE GETS HURT."

< back
next >

NORTHERN
MOCKINGBIRD
(MIMUS POLYGLOTTOS)
HOW TO MA.I.M.
A MOCKINGBIRD
PART THREE
SECRET
AVENGERS

ONEIRIC.
UH...
WELCOME BACK, BARBARA.
YOU MUST BE CONFUSED, SO I WILL EASE YOU INTO THIS.
MY NAME IS ANDREW FORSON. I JUST USED A TRIGGER WORD. THIS TRIGGER WORD WILL GRADUALLY HELP YOU RECALL YOUR TRUE IDENTITY.
YOU ARE A SECRET AGENT. YOU'VE WORKED FOR THE CULT OF ENTROPY FOR A VERY LONG TIME NOW.
IF IT HELPS...
...IF IT HELPS, IMAGINE THE DEEPEST MEMORIES THAT WILL BE FLOATING TO THE SURFACE OF YOUR MIND AS MONOCHROMATIC. AS YOU GET CLOSER TO WHERE YOU ARE NOW, THEY CAN FIND A DIFFERENT COLOR...YOU ALWAYS LOVED BLUE, DIDN'T YOU?
I AM TOLD IT HELPS TO BRING UP PAST EVENTS SO ONE CAN COME BACK...FULLY.
BUT OUR TIME IS RATHER LIMITED. I'LL GET STRAIGHT TO THE POINT.
WHAT DO YOU REMEMBER, MOCKINGBIRD?

A.I.M. ISLAND.
A LONG TIME AGO.
MY NAME IS...
...MY NAME IS BARBARA MORSE.

CAN YOU TURN IT OFF?

NO. YOU KNOW AS WELL AS I DO THAT THERE'S NO GOING BACK FROM THIS.

YOU SAID YOU ARE PSYCHIC.
WHY ARE YOU INTERESTED IN BEING INITIATED INTO THE CULT OF ENTROPY?

BECAUSE IT'S THE RIGHT THING TO DO. IT'S THE BEST WAY.

DO YOU SEE ENTROPY AS THE FINAL AND ABSOLUTE GOAL?

...
YES.

YOU CLAIMED YOU CAN "FEEL" THE FUTURE.
IS THIS CORRECT?
YES.
IS ENTROPY THE FINAL STATE? IS THIS THE FUTURE WE ARE MOVING TOWARDS?

YES.

WHAT DID YOU SEE IN YOUR VISIONS, BARBARA?

I SAW THE END.

DO YOU WANT TO CONTRIBUTE TO IT?

YES.

WHY?
BECAUSE ENTROPY IS THE KEY.
THE KEY TO WHAT?

TO EXISTENCE.

DO YOU ACCEPT THE POSSIBLE CONSEQUENCES OF YOUR ACTIONS?

YES.

COME BACK.
BARBARA.
COME BACK.
UHHHH...
WHAT HAVE I DONE?

A.I.M. SUBMARINE.
DEEP UNDERWATER.
CARE TO SHARE OUR IMMINENT DESTINATION WITH US, BELOVA?
WHY NOT.
BACK TO A.I.M. ISLAND, OF COURSE.
AND THEN?
YOU WILL BE SHOT, AGENT FURY.
WILL YOU TEND TO MY WOUND, YELENA?
YES. WITH A WELDING TORCH.
J'ADORE.
Page TURNS AR

FURY. NATASHA
WE COULD TAK
THEM NOW.

FIFTEEN MINUTES LATER.

TH OUR HANDS AND LEGS CUFFED. URE, BARTON. BECAUSE WE'RE A BUNCH OF SUPER HEROES.

I NEVER D I'M A SUPER HERO.

BUT IF--

I AM MOST CERTAINLY NOT A SUPER HERO.

--IF SOMEONE LLED ME THAT, I OULDN'T OBJ--

IF SOMEONE CALLED ME THAT, I WOULD MOST CERTAINLY--

DID ANYONE CONSIDER THE OBVIOUS?

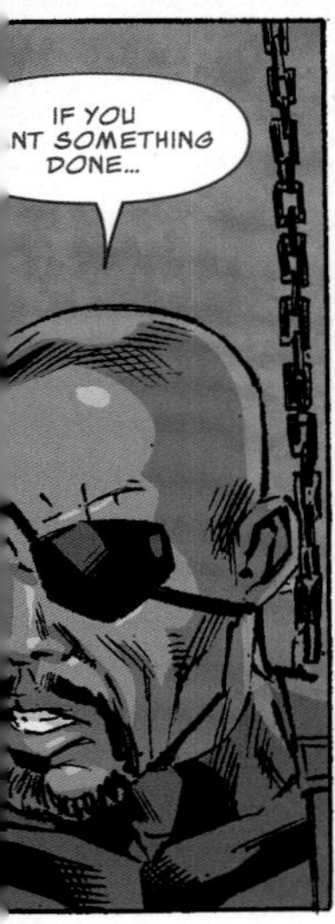


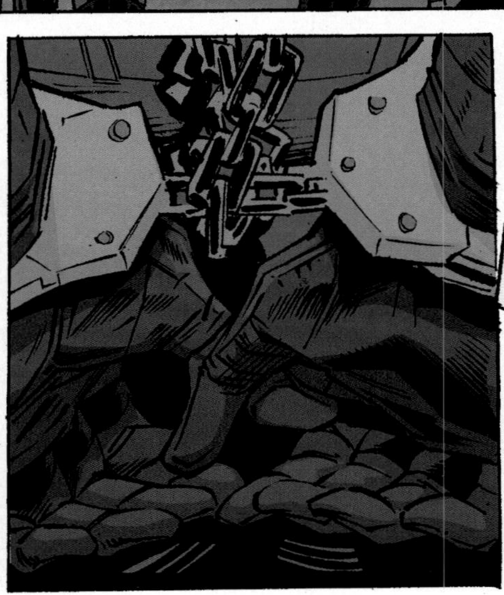

ONEIRIC.

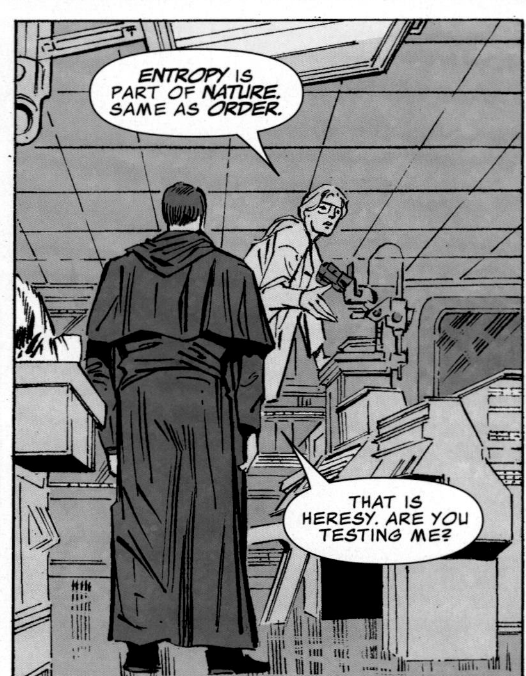
ENTROPY IS PART OF NATURE. SAME AS ORDER.
THAT IS HERESY. ARE YOU TESTING ME?

NO. THAT IS SCIENCE. I AM MERELY STATING A FACT.
BUT YOU KNOW HOW THIS ENDS.

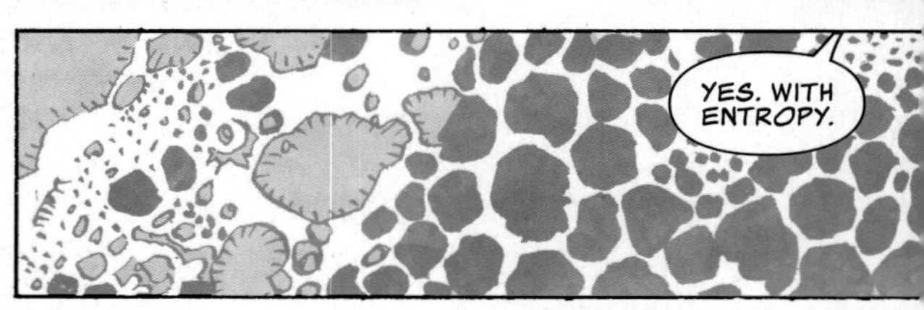
YES. WITH ENTROPY.

AND CHAOS. THE DARKNESS AT THE HEART OF IT ALL.

AND FROM CHAOS...

UGH.

WHAT IS IT?

UNNHHH...
WHAT IS IT, BARBARA?
THAT TIME I DROPPED THE MICROSCOPE.
DON'TTALK TOHIM.
I WANT TO TALK TO HIM.
I DROPPED A MICROSCOPE AND WE CAUGHT SOMEONE. WE CAUGHT SOMEONE HERE. ON THE ISLAND.
OH.
YES.
THAT WAS SHORTLY AFTER YOU STARTED WORKING FOR US...WHEN VICTORIUS WAS RUNNING THE CULT. DO YOU REMEMBER VICTORIUS?
NO? OH, WELL. I THOUGHT HE WAS PRETTY MEMORABLE, ANYWAY.
YOU WERE ALREADY WORKING FOR ME BACK THEN. HE HAD NO IDEA...

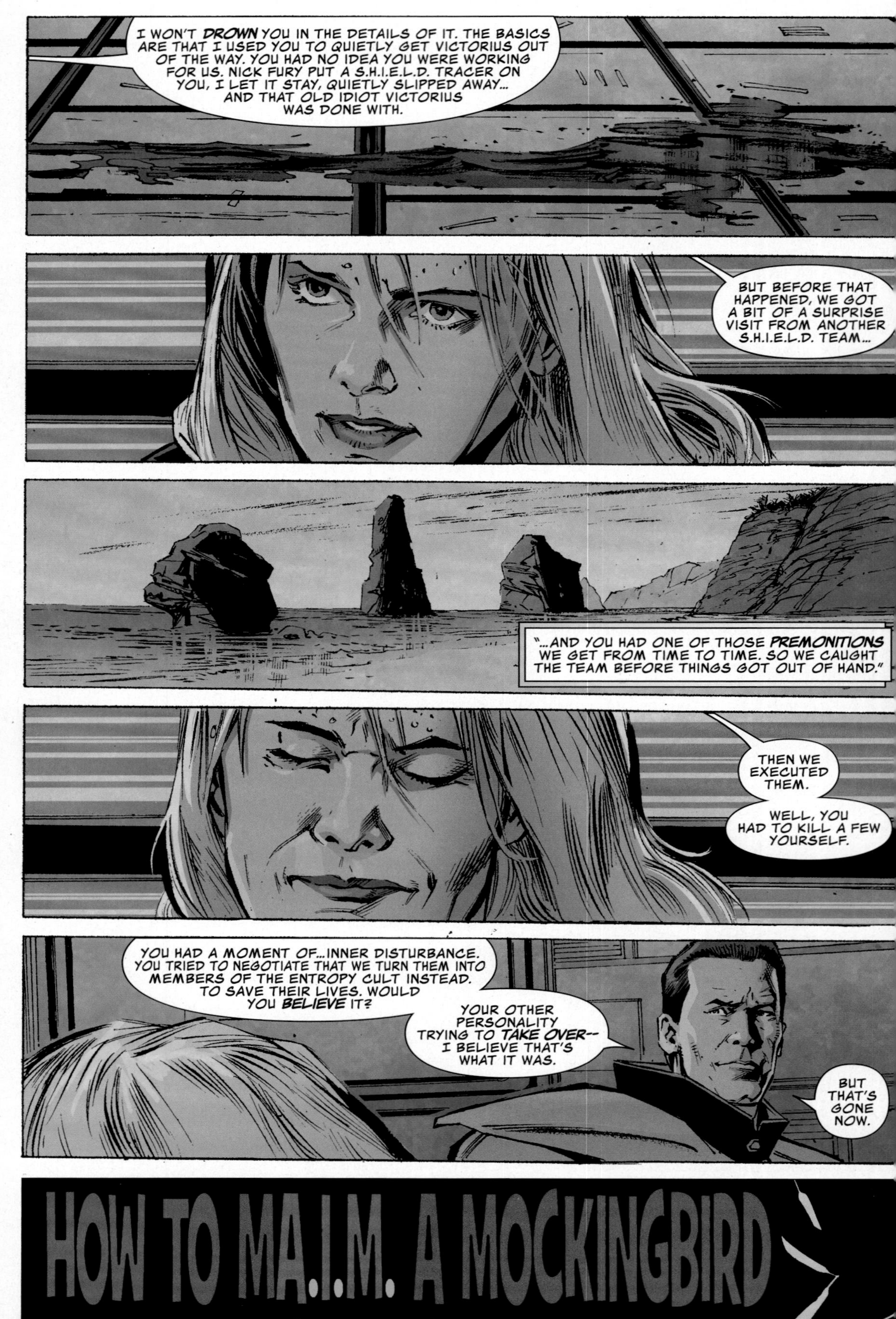
I WON'T DROWN YOU IN THE DETAILS OF IT. THE BASICS ARE THAT I USED YOU TO QUIETLY GET VICTORIUS OUT OF THE WAY. YOU HAD NO IDEA YOU WERE WORKING FOR US. NICK FURY PUT A S.H.I.E.L.D. TRACER ON YOU, I LET IT STAY, QUIETLY SLIPPED AWAY... AND THAT OLD IDIOT VICTORIUS WAS DONE WITH.
BUT BEFORE THAT HAPPENED, WE GOT A BIT OF A SURPRISE VISIT FROM ANOTHER S.H.I.E.L.D. TEAM...
"...AND YOU HAD ONE OF THOSE PREMONITIONS WE GET FROM TIME TO TIME. SO WE CAUGHT THE TEAM BEFORE THINGS GOT OUT OF HAND."
THEN WE EXECUTED THEM.
WELL, YOU HAD TO KILL A FEW YOURSELF.
YOU HAD A MOMENT OF...INNER DISTURBANCE. YOU TRIED TO NEGOTIATE THAT WE TURN THEM INTO MEMBERS OF THE ENTROPY CULT INSTEAD. TO SAVE THEIR LIVES. WOULD YOU BELIEVE IT?
YOUR OTHER PERSONALITY TRYING TO TAKE OVER-- I BELIEVE THAT'S WHAT IT WAS.
BUT THAT'S GONE NOW.
HOW TO MA.I.M. A MOCKINGBIRD
PART THREE OF FIVE

THESE ARE THE FIFTEEN TARGETED AREAS.

S.H.I.E.L.D. HELICARRIER *ILIAD*. INTERROGATION ROOM.

THERE IS ALSO THE MATTER OF A HUGE WEAPONS DELIVERY HAPPENING NEXT WEEK NEAR ZAGREB, CROATIA.

THE MAN YOU ARE LOOKING FOR IS ARTAUD DERRIDA. HE'S A FAILED POET. NOWADAYS HE BELIEVES IN HARD CASH AND IMPRESSIONABLE LIT STUDENTS.

M.O.D.O.K. ENJOYS ICE CREAM. DO YOU HAVE ICE CREAM?

WE HAVE A LONG NIGHT AHEAD OF US--
HILL. I GAVE YOU A WAY TO KILL PLENTY OF MEN AND WOMEN WHO ARE OPPOSED TO YOUR INTERESTS.
GIVE ME ICE CREAM.
*OUR* INTERESTS. AND YOU'RE STILL TRYING THE CUTE ROUTINE. IT WON'T GET YOU ANYWHERE.
GIVE ME MORE *DATA.*
THIS IS NO WAY TO TREAT A BUSINESSMAN.

THAT OTHER PERSON. BOBBI. I WANT HER GONE.
GONE FROM MY HEAD. SHE'S TRYING TO STAY.
NO WORRIES. THE SECONDARY IDENTITY WILL LEAVE SOONER OR LATER. YOUR PLACE IS HERE, WITH US.

NOW PLEASE CONTINUE

ELSEWHERE ON A.I.M. ISLAND.

HI.

I AM SORRY TO DISTURB YOU, MINISTER MENTALLO.

HOWEVER, MAY I ASK...

...WHAT ARE YOU DOING IN THE MORGUE?

I'M MEDITATING.

WHO DIED TODAY?

MINISTER TASKMASTER. IT IS BELIEVED HE WAS A TRAITOR.

AW, MAN...

I BELIEVE THIS IS THE WAY, YES.

SO YOU ARE NOT IN THIS FOR THE MONEY?

BECAUSE YOU CAN BE *HONEST* WITH ME.

I WOULD NEVER *HURT* YOU.

ANDREW...

I UNDERSTAND THAT THIS MIGHT BE HARD TO HEAR, BUT YOU ARE NOT NEARLY AS *SECURE* AS YOU WANT TO LOOK.

WHATEVER HAPPENED TO YOU--

"...YOU ALREADY KNOW A THING OR TWO ABOUT THAT, DON'T YOU?"

I'M SORRY.

LET'S PUT THIS ON PAUSE FOR NOW.
MINISTER BELOVA HAS ARRIVED... AND SHE BROUGHT A FEW MEMBERS OF THE GROUP YOUR FAKE SELF WORKED FOR.

DO YOU FEEL LIKE EXECUTING SOME PEOPLE AGAIN, BARBARA?
NOTHING LIKE A LITTLE EXERCISE TO GET THE REFLEXES BACK AND FLOWING, RIGHT?

SURE.
WHY NOT?

A.I.M. ISLAND.
SUBMARINE DOCK 7A.
I BET WIDOW WOULD PAY GOOD MONEY TO BE THE ONE TO DO THIS.
DO WHAT?
THIS.
KRAANK

SECRET AVENGERS...

...LET'S END THIS.

HAZARD
INTERVENTION
ESPIONAGE
LOGISTICS
back
next

HOW TO MA.I.M.
A MOCKINGBIRD
PART FOUR
SECRET
AVENGERS

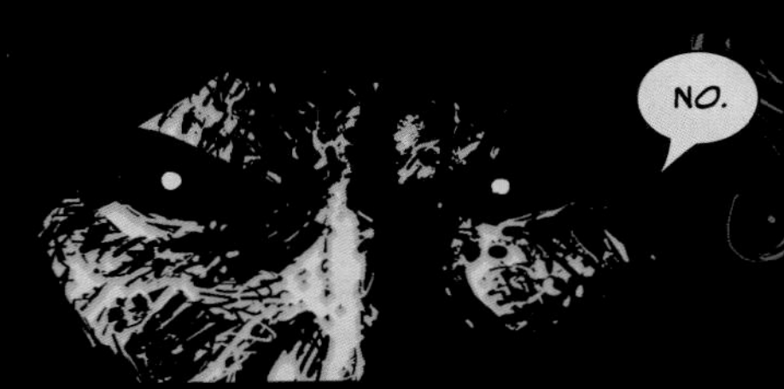

# HOW TO MA.I.M. A MOCKINGBIRD

## PART FOUR OF FIVE

S.H.I.E.L.D.
HELICARRIER *ILIAD.*

"THAT IS EVERYTHING I KNOW, DIRECTOR HILL."

THANK YOU FOR YOUR TIME, M.O.D.O.K.*

*S.H.I.E.L.D. ARCHIVES: MENTAL ORGANISM DESIGNGED ONLY FOR KILLING. OF COURSE.

IS THAT IT?

I WOULD LIKE TO SIGN **THE BINDING AGREEMENT** NOW.

THAT WON'T HAPPEN. I JUST USED YOU.

...

WE DID.
NOT.
ENOUGH.
I WILL GIVE YOU WHAT YOU WANT.
BUT FIRST, I WILL SIGN A CONTRACT THAT WILL GRANT ME AND MY TEAM A LAB. AND IMMUNITY.
WE WANT TO MAKE SCIENCE FOR S.H.I.E.L.D.

A.I.M. ISLAND.

IMPOSSIBLE!

IS JUST A WORD!

THE ONE WE ARRIVED IN? YES. YOU CAN.
BOOT
KLUNK
...I PREFER "ACHIEVEMENT."

GETS IN OR OUT. UNDERSTAND?
YES, SIR.
HOW COULD YOU LET THEM ESCAPE?!
WHAT DO YOU MEAN "CAN'T REACH THE MINISTERS"?
DR. ANDREW FORSON, A.I.M. SCIENTIST SUPREME.
LOOK, JUST SHUT UP. I'LL BE RIGHT THERE.

WHUMMP

HAVE TO DO EVERYTHING *MYSELF*.

HAWKEYE TO FURY. THE DIVERSION WORKED. I HAVE MOCKINGBIRD. BUT TASKMASTER IS DEAD.
I REPEAT.
TASKMASTER IS DEAD.
WIDOW. ARE WE PROCEEDING WITH THE PLAN?
SURE...
...ALL THAT'S LEFT IS A SHANG-CHI ADAPTOID TO CONVERT TO OUR CAUSE.

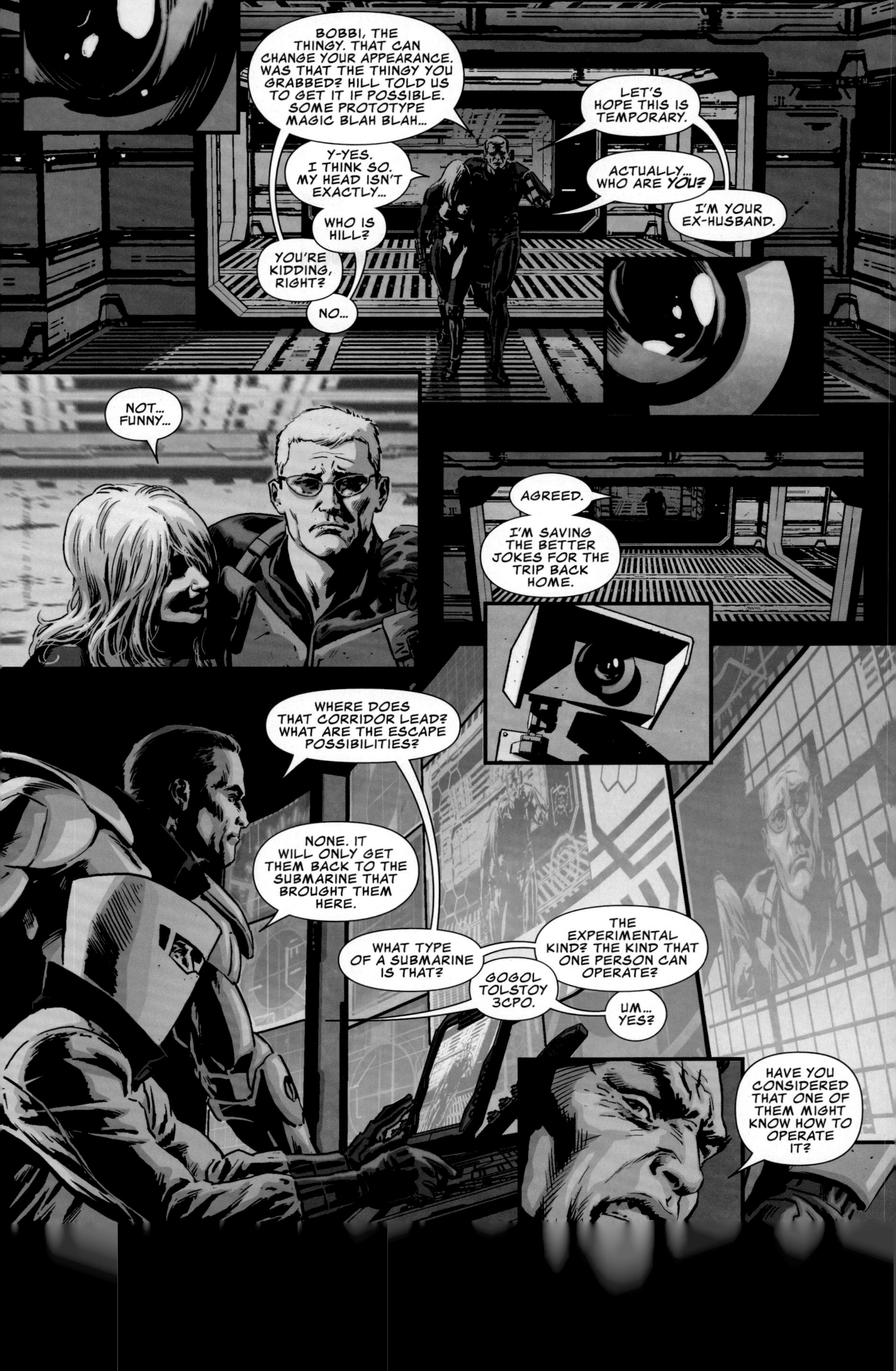
BOBBI, THE THINGY. THAT CAN CHANGE YOUR APPEARANCE. WAS THAT THE THINGY YOU GRABBED? HILL TOLD US TO GET IT IF POSSIBLE. SOME PROTOTYPE MAGIC BLAH BLAH...
Y-YES. I THINK SO. MY HEAD ISN'T EXACTLY...
WHO IS HILL?
YOU'RE KIDDING, RIGHT?
NO...
LET'S HOPE THIS IS TEMPORARY.
ACTUALLY... WHO ARE YOU?
I'M YOUR EX-HUSBAND.
NOT... FUNNY...
AGREED.
I'M SAVING THE BETTER JOKES FOR THE TRIP BACK HOME.
WHERE DOES THAT CORRIDOR LEAD? WHAT ARE THE ESCAPE POSSIBILITIES?
NONE. IT WILL ONLY GET THEM BACK TO THE SUBMARINE THAT BROUGHT THEM HERE.
WHAT TYPE OF A SUBMARINE IS THAT?
THE EXPERIMENTAL KIND? THE KIND THAT ONE PERSON CAN OPERATE?
GOGOL TOLSTOY 3CPO.
UM... YES?
HAVE YOU CONSIDERED THAT ONE OF THEM MIGHT KNOW HOW TO OPERATE IT?

DO YOUR BEST. IT WILL BE WORTH NOTHING.
YOUR FISTS ARE WEAK FLESH. YOUR BONES ARE TWIGS. YOUR FIGHTING STYLES ARE SOULLESS IMITATIONS.
YEAH, YEAH.
TALK TO THE METAL.

GROOVY.
THIS WASN'T SUPPOSED TO HAPPEN.
AT LEAST THIS ADAPTOID HAS A SELF-DESTRUCT MECHANISM...IT'LL TAKE 'EM WITH IT.
YOU MEAN...KILL THEM?
YEAH, OR AT LEAST RIP OFF A FEW LIMBS.
MENTALLO.
A.I.M.'S MINISTER OF PUBLIC AFFAIRS.
FIRE IN THE HO--

HAWKEYE, EVERYTHING ALL RIGHT?
NOT REALLY. BOBBI DOESN'T REMEMBER ME.
GOOD FOR HER.
NOT FUNNY.
DARLING. ARE YOU OKAY?
SORRY. YOU ARE FAMILIAR. I'M HAVING A VERY BAD HEADACHE.
IT'S OKAY. BEING AROUND HAWKEYE FOR TOO LONG TENDS TO DO THAT.
LET'S GET OUT OF HERE.
IT IS VITAL THAT YOU GET MORSE FIRST. SHE KNOWS TOO MUCH. ONLY THEN KILL THE REST.
BARBARA... I WISH THERE WAS ANOTHER WAY.

YOU ARE GOING NOWHERE.
WEAPONS ON THE GROUND. OR MORSE GETS IT.
DON'T SHOOT YET. WE MIGHT HAVE THE SITUATION UNDER CONTROL.
BELOVA IS *MAGNIFICENT,* ISN'T SHE...?
WHOEVER YOU ARE...
...THIS WAS A VERY DUMB IDEA.

AAAAH
DO IT!
BLAM
BLAM
BLAM
BLAM
BLAM
BLAM

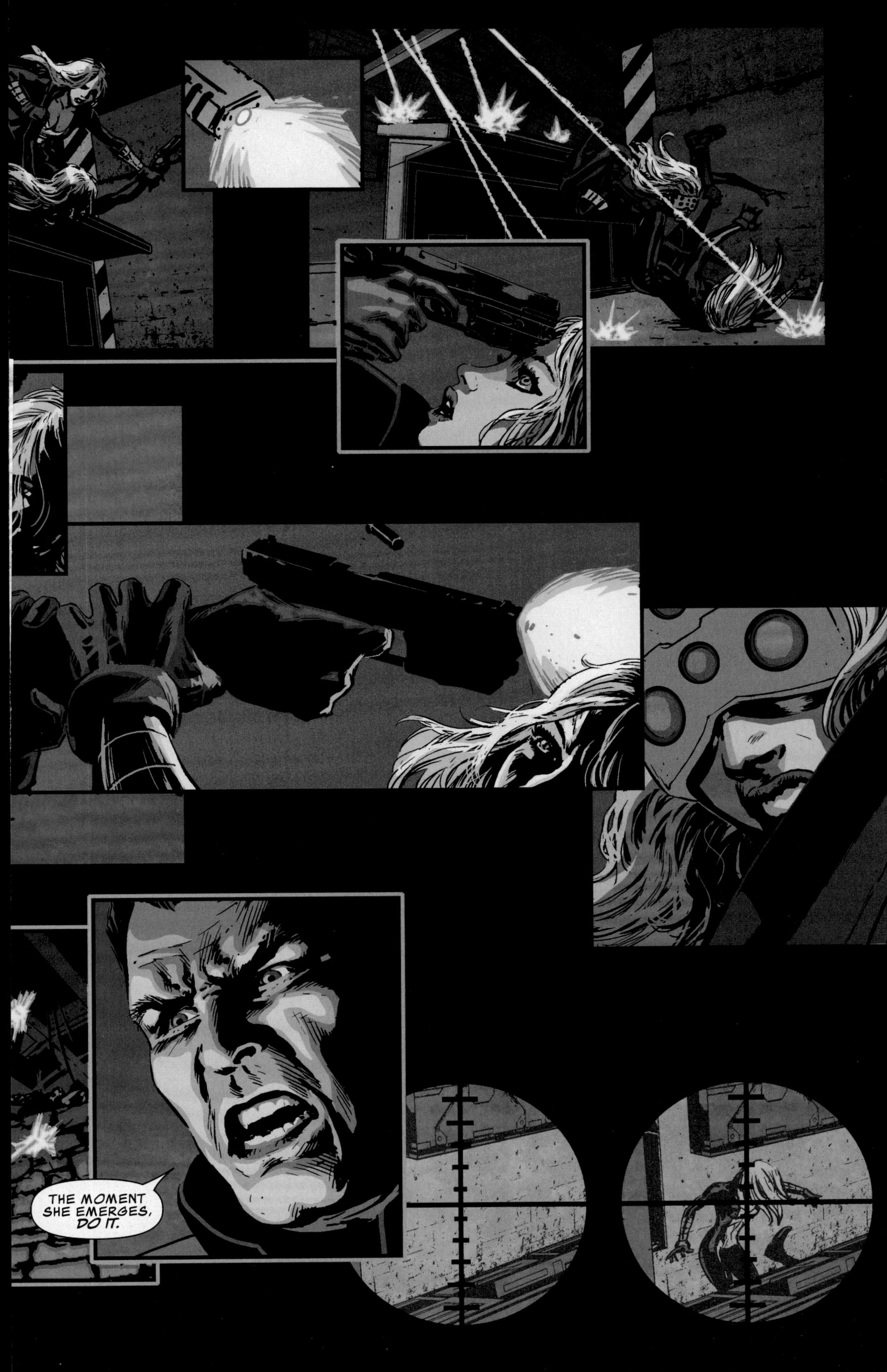
THE MOMENT SHE EMERGES, DO IT.

BOBBI!

KILL THEM!

BOBBI...
CAMOTECH DISENGAGED.

...BOBBI?

HOW TO MA.I.M.
A MOCKINGBIRD
CONCLUSION
SECRET
AVENGERS

A.I.M. ISLAND.
DR. ANDREW FORSON.
A.I.M. SCIENTIST SUPREME.
INCOMING CALL
COMMANDER BELOVA. GOOD JOB.
COMMANDER BELOVA, DO YOU COPY?
YELENA?

HELL.
OPERATOR 6. IS ANYONE IN PURSUIT OF THAT DAMN SUB?
THEY TORPEDOED ALL FOUR VESSELS WE SENT AFTER THEM, SCIENTIST SUPREME.
WHERE THE HELL ARE THE MINISTERS?
WE HAVE NO IDEA, SCIENTIST SUPREME.
I WANT A KILL SQUAD READY BY 2200 HOURS. SIX OF OUR BEST.

DO EVERYTHING MYSELF...
DO EVERYTHING MYSELF, IDIOTS.
SIR.
WE ARE GETTING REPORTS OF MULTIPLE A.I.M. BASES GOING DARK.
WHAT?
AND...
...IT SEEMS THAT OUR SLEEPER AGENTS WITHIN THE S.H.I.E.L.D. ORGANIZATION ARE BEING ARRESTED.
I'LL BE IN THE OPERATIONS CENTER. PREPARE A PRESENTATION. IMMEDIATELY. FIND EVERYONE.
ANDREW.

DO YOU THINK THIS IS HOW HITLER FELT BEFORE HE TOOK THE POISON?
NNGGG.
JUST STAY RIGHT WHERE YOU ARE.
HOW DID YOU--
YOUR AMATEURS LEFT THE IMAGE INDUCER ON THE TABLE. I STUCK IT--NNGGG-- I STUCK IT ON BELOVA.
AMAZING.
I APPLAUD YOUR DECISION. KILLING ME...WAS THE SAFE CHOICE. YOU WEREN'T SURE WHICH "ME" WAS IN CHARGE.
BARBARA--THE HEADACHES WILL GO AWAY IN A FEW WEEKS.
JUST GO WITH THE FLOW. LET THE REAL YOU TAKE OVER.
I GET IT.

YOU KNOW THIS IS WHAT YOU WANT.
DON'T YOU GET IT?
YOU JUST HAVE TO WAKE UP. SEE WHAT'S BEST FOR YOU.
WAKE UP, BARBARA.
ONEIRIC.
THE TRIGGER WORD ISN'T NECESSARY. I FEEL LIKE...
...THERE ARE TWO HALVES OF ME NOW, YOU KNOW?
BUT I CAN SEE CLEARLY... THEY BOTH SEE...A COMMON GROUND... SAYING...SIMILAR THINGS...
YES? THAT'S GOOD. GOOD GIRL. WHAT DOES THE COMMON GROUND SAY?

IT SAYS @&!# YOUR MANSPLAINING!
YOU THINK YOU CAN KILL ME?
YOU THINK YOU CAN TRY THAT...
...AND LIVE?
I
AM
SORRY.

YEAH. I BET YOU ARE.
NGGGHHH--
WHERE AM I--
ARRRGG!

ELSEWHERE ON A.I.M. ISLAND.
Dear Taskmaster.
You are probably very surprised to be reading this.
The truth is, I don't know how you are alive.
I believe it has something to do with the bullet missing all of your vitals.
:GASP:
I believe that whoever shot you either failed miserably or shot you this way hoping you would survive.
Either way, I am perplexed. But that is okay. You were still a vegetable. But how much do we really know about vegetables? Maybe their lives are wonderful and full of experiences.

I'm really glad you're alive.

I was ready to try and fix you with--do you remember when I mentioned the nanobots?

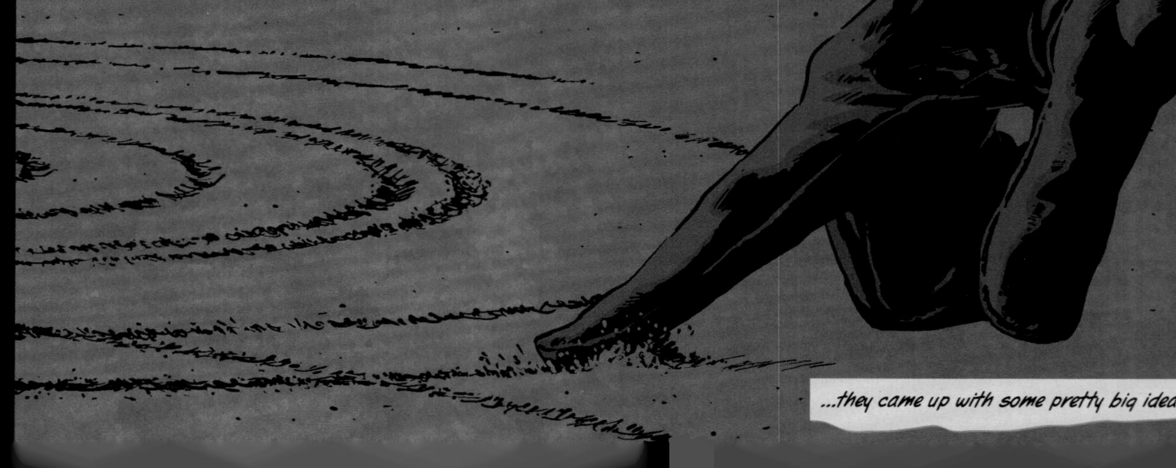

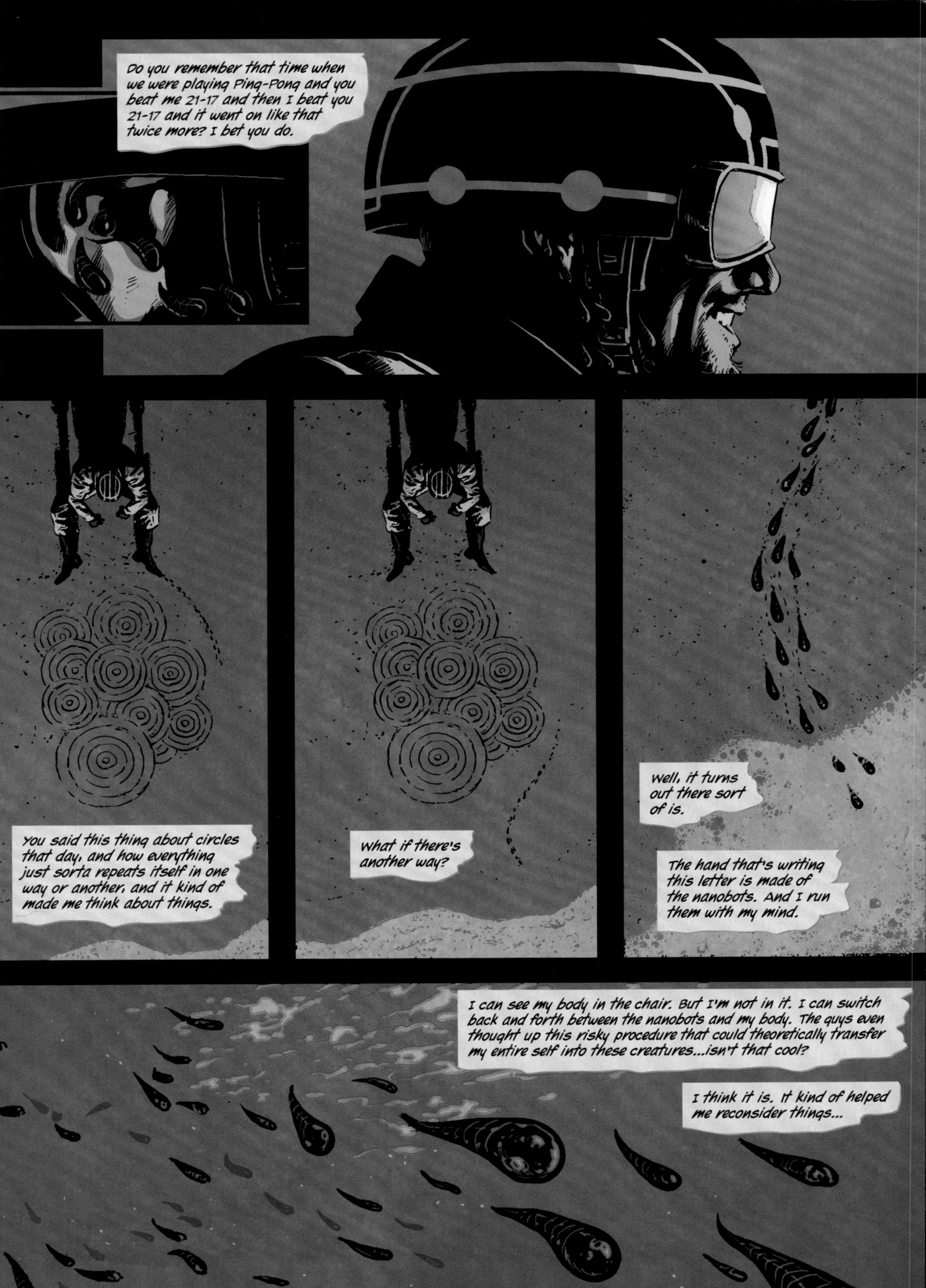
Do you remember that time when we were playing Ping-Pong and you beat me 21-17 and then I beat you 21-17 and it went on like that twice more? I bet you do.
You said this thing about circles that day, and how everything just sorta repeats itself in one way or another, and it kind of made me think about things.
What if there's another way?
Well, it turns out there sort of is.
The hand that's writing this letter is made of the nanobots. And I run them with my mind.
I can see my body in the chair. But I'm not in it. I can switch back and forth between the nanobots and my body. The guys even thought up this risky procedure that could theoretically transfer my entire self into these creatures...isn't that cool?
I think it is. It kind of helped me reconsider things...

...and I always loved the ocean.
Goodbye, my friend.
See you around.

S.H.I.E.L.D. HELICARRIER ILIAD.
ALL THE EQUIPMENT I WILL ASK FOR, FREE SUNDAYS, SEVEN ASSISTANTS, SCRAMBLED EGGS AND BACON EVERY MORNING EXCEPT FOR THURSDAYS, I PREFER OATMEAL AND GRAPEFRUIT JUICE THEN...
AND NO NEED TO PAY ME. I'VE MADE ENOUGH FOR A FEW LIFETIMES ALREADY. DID YOU KNOW THAT I HAVE MY OWN ISLAND?
TWO ASSISTANTS. AND THERE'S NO WAY IN HELL YOU'RE GETTING FREE SUNDAYS. OR BREAKFASTS LIKE THAT.
ONE SOMETIMES HAS TO PUSH AGAINST THE LIMITS IN ORDER TO ACHIEVE GREATNESS, DIRECTOR HILL.
LET'S MAKE THIS CLEAR, M.O.D.O.K.*: I KNOW THAT YOU HAVE AN AGENDA YOU ARE NOT TELLING ME ABOUT.
*MENTAL ORGANISM DESIGNED ONLY FOR KILLING...SURE.
RIGHT NOW, I DON'T KNOW WHAT IT IS.
BUT I WILL FIND OUT.
AND I WILL HAVE YOUR ASS ON A PLATTER.

AND I SWEAR, IF YOU TRY TO CROSS ME, OR HURT ANY OF MY EMPLOYEES...
MY AGENDA IS TO SURVIVE.
THAT'S WHY I GAVE YOU THE OFFER AND THAT'S WHY I SIGNED UP WITH YOU AND S.H.I.E.L.D.
SOMETIMES YOU JUST HAVE TO KNOW WHEN YOU'VE LOST. AND I DO.
I SURRENDER BECAUSE IT'S THE SMARTEST OPTION.
AND BECAUSE YOU AND I...WE ARE VERY SIMILAR.
I FIND SOLACE IN THAT.

I QUIT.
FINE.
JUST LIKE THAT?
YES, HAWKEYE. CONSIDERING THE CIRCUMSTANCES, I UNDERSTAND.
I AM SORRY FOR WHAT HAPPENED. WE WILL FIND HER.
UM, MARIA...
YES, RHODEY?
..I WAS ACTUALLY THINKING I'M GOING TO STEP AWAY AS WELL. THE MISSIONS YOU GIVE US, THE LACK OF OVERSIGHT...WHY WAS FURY THE ONLY ONE ON THE ENTIRE MISSION WITH THE INTEL ON MOCKINGBIRD'S CAPTURE? I FEEL I SHOULD...
ANYONE ELSE?

...FINE.
RHODEY, BARTON...I AM OKAY WITH YOU GOING. THE OPERATION WILL HAVE TO CHANGE ANYWAY, AND RADICALLY SO.
BUT BEFORE THAT HAPPENS, I HAVE ONE MORE THING TO SAY.
REVER

# HOW TO MA.I.M. A MOCKINGBIRD

## PART FIVE OF FIVE

WELCOME.
WE WERE BORED. WE WORKED OUT.
BUCKY BARNES, a.k.a.
THE WINTER SOLDIER.
DAISY JOHNSON
a.k.a. QUAKE
EX-S.H.I.E.L.D.
BOBBI, MEET MARTHA. MARTHA, MEET BOBBI.
HI. NICE TO MEET YOU.
HI. I'M SO SORRY ABOUT THE MESS.
ALSO I'M FAMISHED.
THE COPS WILL BE HERE SOON. EAT FAST.

WHAT'S THE PLAN?
WHAT WAS IN THE SUITCASE?
I DON'T KNOW.
NAZI MONEY. MARTHA SAID SHE ALWAYS WANTED TO GO TO HAWAII, SO WE THOUGHT, HEY, WHY NOT GIVE THE LADY A NICE GIFT AND TELL HER TO GET LOST BEFORE THE COPS GET HERE...
I'VE NEVER BEEN TO HAWAII.
ARE YOU SAYING WE SHOULD GO TO HAWAII WITH MARTHA?
I'M SAYING...
...WE'RE FREE AGENTS.
WE CAN GO WHEREVER WE WANT.

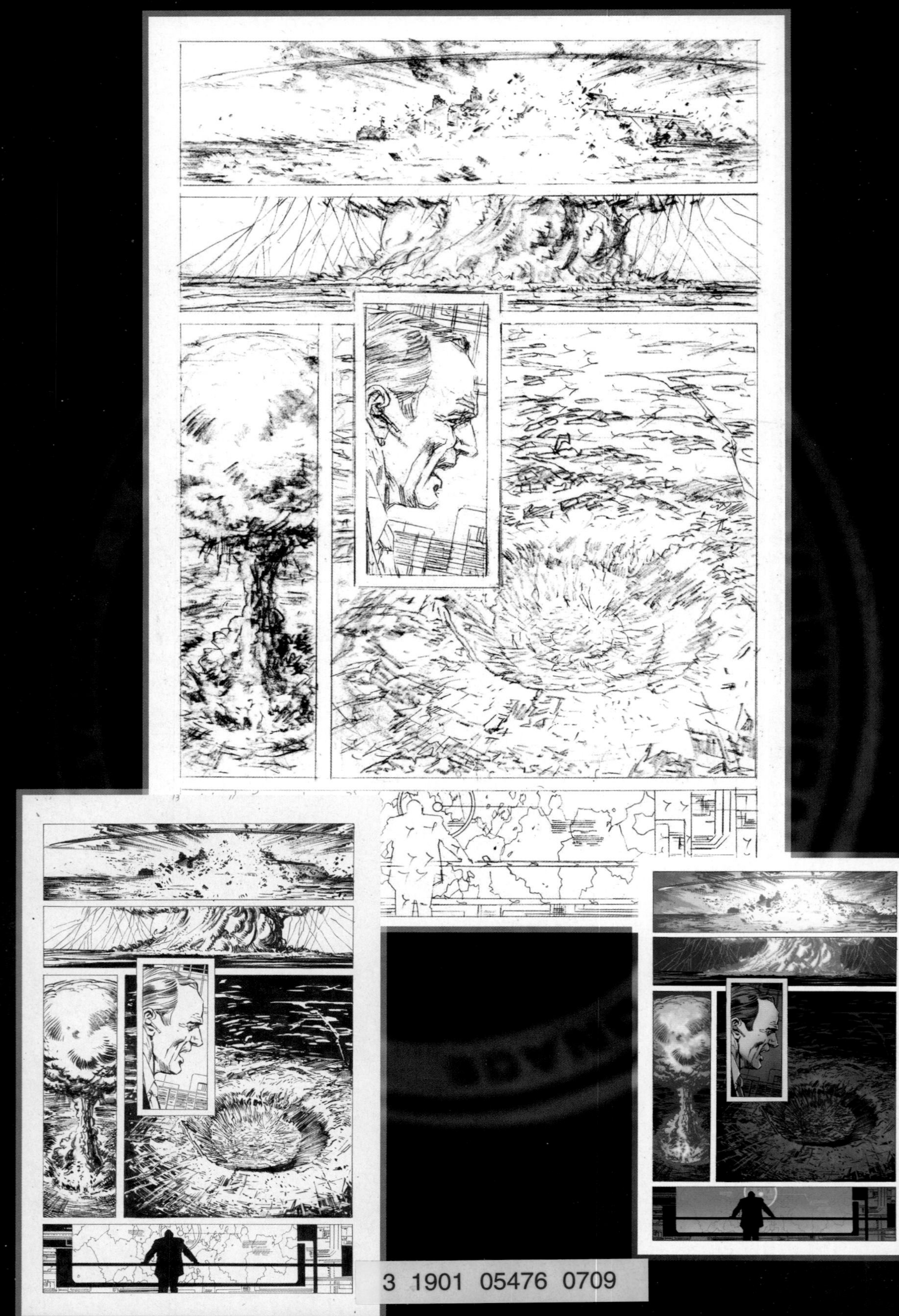



**SECRET AVENGERS #13, PAGE 11**

ART PROCESS | BY BUTCH GUICE, JOE RUBINSTEIN & MATTHEW WILSON